CENGAGE Learning

Short Stories for Students, Volume 35

Project Editor: Sara Constantakis Rights Acquisition and Management: Jacqueline Flowers, Robyn Young Composition: Evi Abou-El-Seoud Manufacturing: Rhonda A. Dover Imaging: John Watkins

Product Design: Pamela A. E. Galbreath, Jennifer Wahi Content Conversion: Katrina Coach Product Manager: Meggin Condino © 2012 Gale, Cengage Learning publisher.

Since this page cannot legibly accommodate all copyright notices, the acknowledgments constitute an extension of the copyright notice.

For product information and technology assistance, contact us at **Gale Customer Support, 1-800-877-4253**.

For permission to use material from this text or product, submit all requests online at **www.cengage.com/permissions**.

Further permissions questions can be emailed to **permissionrequest@cengage.com** While every effort has been made to ensure the reliability of the information presented in this publication, Gale, a part of Cengage Learning, does not guarantee the accuracy of the data contained herein. Gale accepts no payment for listing; and inclusion in the publication of any organization, agency, institution, publication, service, or individual does not imply endorsement of the editors or publisher. Errors brought to the attention of the publisher and verified to the satisfaction of the publisher will be corrected in future editions.

Gale
27500 Drake Rd.
Farmington Hills, MI, 48331-3535

ISBN-13: 978-1-4144-8740-3
ISBN-10: 1-4144-8740-1
ISSN 1092-7735

This title is also available as an e-book.
ISBN-13: 978-1-4144-8743-4

ISBN-10: 1-4144-8743-6
Contact your Gale, a part of Cengage Learning sales
representative for ordering information.

Printed in Mexico
1 2 3 4 5 6 7 15 14 13 12

The Homecoming

Harold Pinter

1965

Introduction

The Homecoming, now considered by many critics
to be Harold Pinter's masterpiece, was not
universally admired when it was first produced in
England by the Royal Shakespeare Company at
London's Aldwych Theatre, on June 3, 1965. Many
critics, while praising the production directed by
Peter Hall, found the play itself to be baffling and
enigmatic in the extreme. Harold Hobson, critic for
the *Sunday Times* and an early proponent of

Pinter's, predicted that the play would "suffer in the estimation of audiences who will perceive an aesthetic defect that does not exist, in the place of a moral vacuum that does." Despite numerous viewer reactions that verified Hobson's forecast, *The Homecoming* had a long run to packed houses in London before moving to the United States.

The Broadway opening of *The Homecoming* on January 3, 1967, at the Music Box Theatre was greeted with great excitement. Repeating its London success, the production had a long run in spite of some negative reviews, the most notable by Walter Kerr of the *New York Times*. In March *The Homecoming* won the Antionette ("Tony") Perry Award as best play on Broadway and in May it was voted best new play on Broadway by the New York Drama Critics' Circle. It also received the Whitbread Anglo-American award for the best British play of the year. This sensational success established Pinter's reputation in New York, opening the door to widespread production of his subsequent work.

While baffled by the fact that the startling action of the play seemed to lack any *rational* explanations, both critics and audiences responded to Pinter's gift for dramatic suspense and sharp, biting comedy. *The Homecoming* does in fact deal with many themes, such as emotional impotence, Oedipal desires, personal loneliness and isolation, appearance and reality, and familial power struggles, to mention a few; and, audiences and critics alike sensed that there is a great deal more going on in the play than can be easily articulated. As John Russell Taylor put it in *Plays and Players* magazine, "The secret of the play does not lie in our providing a neat crossword-puzzle solution." Despite—and perhaps because of—the play's ambiguity, *The Homecoming* has remained a centerpiece in Pinter's canon. New productions of the play are frequent as actors, directors, and audiences attempt new interpretations of Pinter's work.

Author Biography

Harold Pinter was born in the northern borough of Hackney, a working-class section in London, England, on October 10, 1930. Pinter's father, Hyman (Jack) was a hard-working tailor of women's apparel and his mother, Frances, a homemaker. The Pinter family was part of the immigrant wave of Jews that arrived in London around the turn of the century. Pinter's forebears came from Poland and Odessa and brought with them a love of culture and learning. At the outbreak of World War II in 1939, Pinter was evacuated to a castle in Cornwall for a year where, away from his loving home for the first time, he suffered loneliness, bewilderment, separation, and loss— themes that recur in all his works. He also discovered just how sly and nasty a group of boys isolated from their families could be. Back in Hackney, where he spent most of the war years, he was constantly made aware of the impermanence of life.

Pinter attended Hackney Downs Grammar School from 1944 to 1948, where his talents were inspired by Joe Brearley, an English teacher. Pinter wrote for the school magazine and discovered a flair for acting in school productions. He also was one of a group who called themselves "The Boys," a sort of gang tied together by their common love for intellectual adventure. Along with other boyish pursuits, the group would often gather and argue about literature. Although the Boys were not immune from the desire for domination and the clashes brought about by sexual competition, many remained friends throughout their adult lives.

On leaving school, Pinter received a grant to study acting at the Royal Academy of Dramatic Art, but he soon became disenchanted with the academic process and left after two terms. In 1948 he was called up for national military service and declared himself a conscientious objector, a status that was denied him. He was tried and expected to go to prison but instead was fined thirty pounds by a sympathetic magistrate and released. In 1951 he resumed his acting education at the Central School of Speech and Drama. He then spent eighteen months touring Ireland with the theatrical company of Anew McMaster followed by the 1953 London season with the company of Donald Wolfit. Following this activity, he took on the stage name David Baron and began acting in provincial repertory theatres. During this acting stint, Pinter met actress Vivian Merchant, with whom he often worked. The couple were married in 1956.

On May 9, 1957, one of the Hackney "Boys," Henry Woolfe, asked Pinter to write a play to be produced six days later at Bristol University. Pinter, writing in the afternoons between morning rehearsals and evening performances, completed his first play, *The Room*, in four days. The production was a success and was subsequently entered in the *Sunday Times* student drama festival several months later. Harold Hobson, an influential drama critic for the paper, was so taken with the play that he wrote a highly favorable review.

Hobson's accolade brought Pinter to the attention of Michael Codron, a young London producer, who asked the young actor if he had any other works he'd like to see produced. Pinter sent Codron *The Birthday Party* and *The Dumb Waiter*. The producer staged the former, which opened on April 28, 1958, to generally unfavorable reviews. Hobson, however, reviewed the play in the *Sunday Times* four days after opening night, stating that, based on the evidence of this play, "Mr. Pinter possesses the most original, disturbing, and arresting talent in theatrical London." Despite such strong praise, it was too late to save that production of *The Birthday Party* and the show soon closed. *The Dumb Waiter* later had its first English production, coupled with *The Room*, at the Hampstead Theatre Club in 1960.

By the late 1950s, Pinter was becoming a playwright in increasing demand. The British Broadcasting Corporation (BBC) commissioned Pinter to write a radio drama, a piece he called *Something in Common*, which was not produced. The BBC then commissioned another sixty-minute play, *A Slight Ache* (1959), the first of Pinter's many (produced) plays written for radio or television. Also in 1959, Pinter wrote a series of comic sketches that were included in popular revues. In 1960, Pinter had his first major theatrical success with *The Caretaker*. Pinter, now recognized as an important writer, worked prolifically on his dramas, producing such works as *Night School* (1960), *The Dwarfs* (1960), *The Collection* (1961), *The Lover* (1963), *The Tea Party* (1965), and *The Basement* (1967). He also began working in the medium of film, writing the screenplays for *The Servant* (1963) and *The Pumpkin Eater* (1964), which both received major awards.

The Homecoming, Pinter's third full-length play, was first produced at the New Theatre in Cardiff, Wales, in 1965. Under the auspices of the Royal Shakespeare Company, it moved to the Aldwych Theatre in London later that year. In 1967 the production made its American debut on Broadway at the Music Box Theatre. The play became a sensational success and established Pinter as a significant dramatist in the United States.

Throughout the 1960s, 70s, 80s, and 90s, Pinter has continued to flourish in theatre as a playwright, director (of both his own works and those by other playwrights), and occasionally as an actor. He also continues to write for films, including *The Last Tycoon, The French Lieutenant's Woman* (adapted from the book by John Fowles), and *Turtle Diary*, as well as adaptations of his own plays (including *The Birthday Party, Betrayal*, and *The Homecoming*).

Pinter and Merchant had one child, a son named Daniel, before divorcing in 1980. He remarried later that year, taking the writer Lady Antonia Fraser as his wife. Pinter's work has spanned five decades, and he remains one of the worlds most respected and widely produced playwrights.

Plot Summary

The Homecoming is set in a large room in an old house in working-class North London. This is the home of Max, a retired butcher; Sam, his brother, who drives for a car-hire (cab) service; and two of Max's sons: Lenny, a successful pimp, and Joey, a dullard who works on a demolition crew during the day while trying to become a professional boxer.

Act I, scene 1

The play opens with Lenny reading the newspaper. Max enters looking for scissors and is ignored by Lenny. Max talks about his late wife Jessie and his late friend MacGregor. He speaks of Jessie with both fondness and shocking disapproval: "She wasn't such a bad woman. Even though it made me sick just to look at her rotten stinking face, she wasn't such a bad bitch." Max also talks of his special understanding of horses. Lenny tells Max to shut up and then says that Max's cooking is fit only for dogs. Sam enters and Max insults him about his driving and the fact that he is not married. Joey enters from a workout at the gym, and Max turns on him, saying that his trouble as a boxer is that he doesn't know how to attack or defend himself. Max also threatens to throw Sam out when he is too old to pay his way. Sam pointedly reminds Max that Mac and Jessie were very close friends. The scene ends in blackout.

Act I, scene 2

The next scene, a few hours later, opens with Teddy and Ruth standing at the threshold to the room. Teddy is Max's eldest son, a Ph.D. who teaches philosophy at an American university. Ruth is his wife of six years about whom the rest of the family know nothing. They have been on a trip to Europe, and Teddy has brought her to meet the family. Ruth, though at first claiming to be tired, decides to go out for a walk. After Ruth leaves, Lenny enters. The reunion between the two brothers is civil but without any sense of warmth. Teddy goes to bed and Lenny goes and gets a clock that he suspects of disturbing his sleep.

Ruth enters and after some surprising small talk, says that she is Teddy's wife. Lenny pays no attention to that. He launches into a long story which ends with his beating up a whore, whom he would have killed except for the bother of getting rid of the body. He then tells another long story that ends with his beating up an old woman, Whether true or not, these tales are obviously meant to intimidate Ruth. They do not. There follows a wonderfully theatrical power play with Ruth dominating Lenny by using a glass of water to taunt him with sexual favors. Ruth goes to bed leaving Lenny alone. Max enters and Lenny turns on him asking about the night he was conceived. Max spits at him and says he will drown in his own blood.

Act I, scene 3

The next scene opens at six-thirty the next morning. Joey is working out. Max enters complaining that Sam is in his kitchen. He calls Sam into the room and belittles him. Teddy and Ruth enter, and Max calls Ruth a "smelly scruffer," a "stinking pox-ridden slut," and says that there hasn't been a whore in the house since Jessie died. Ruth seems to be unfazed by this verbal abuse. Joey apologizes for Max, saying he is an old man. Max hits Joey in the stomach with all his might. Joey staggers across the room, and Max begins to collapse with the exertion; Sam tries to help Max, and Max hits him in the head with his cane. Max then asks Ruth if she is a mother, seems pleased when she says she has three boys, and asks Teddy for a cuddle. Teddy accepts.

Act II, scene 1

It is just after dinner on the same day. Ruth serves coffee, and the men smoke cigars. Max praises Ruth and tells her that Jessie was the backbone of the family, that she taught the boys "all the morality they know . . . every single bit of the moral code they live by." Max then berates Sam and complains that he has worked hard all his life to support his brother and his own family—"three bastard sons, a slutbitch of a wife"—and even claims to have suffered the pains of childbirth. After further abusing Sam, Max turns to Teddy and gives his marriage his blessing, saying that Ruth is a charming woman. Sam leaves.

Lenny tries to engage Teddy in philosophical speculation about a table. Teddy refuses to be drawn in. Ruth points out that when she moves her leg her underwear moves with her and that perhaps the fact that her lips move is more important than the words which come through them. After a silence Joey, Max, and Lenny leave to go to the gym. Teddy suggests to Ruth that it is time to return home to America. Ruth seems uninterested. Teddy goes to pack. Lenny enters, and he and Ruth talk about the weather. Then Ruth says that before she went to America she had been a "model for the body," and she seems to have a longing for that life again. Teddy enters.

Lenny and Ruth dance slowly and kiss. Max and Joey enter and Joey delightfully says Ruth is a tart. He grabs her and starts to make love to her on the sofa. Max makes small talk with Teddy and praises Ruth in extremely sentimental terms. Ruth suddenly pushes Joey away, stands up, and demands a drink. She further demands food, that the record be turned off, and that she be given a particular kind of glass. She then asks if the family have read Teddy's critical works. Teddy says that they wouldn't understand them.

Act II, scene 2

The following scene takes place that evening and opens with Teddy in his coat sitting dejectedly with his suitcases beside him. Sam asks if Teddy remembers MacGregor and says that Teddy was always his mother's favorite. When Lenny enters, Sam leaves. Lenny accuses Teddy of stealing his sandwich and is outraged when Teddy admits that he did. Joey enters: he has been in his room with Ruth for two hours but he didn't get "all the way." Max and Sam enter and Max demands, "Where's the whore?" Max commiserates with Joey and says that it might be good to have Ruth stay with them. Teddy says that she should go home to her children. The problem of supporting Ruth is discussed, and Lenny suggests that she could pay her own way by working as a whore. Max, Joey, and Lenny agree that this is a good idea.

When Ruth enters, Teddy explains what the family has in mind. Ruth says, "How very nice of them." Her demands, however, are very specific: a flat with three rooms and a bath, a maid, complete wardrobe, and that the original outlay must be viewed as a capital investment. She demands a contract to be signed before witnesses. All is agreed to. Sam then bursts out with the information that MacGregor had Jessie in the back of Sam's cab as he drove them along. He collapses. No one helps him. Teddy complains that he had counted on Sam to drive him to the airport and leaves to find a cab. Ruth sits in Max's chair, Joey sits on the floor and puts his head in her lap. Max complains that he will be left out, that she thinks he is an old man, and he collapses. As Max crawls toward Ruth, asking her for a kiss, Lenny sullenly stands watching.

Characters

Jessie

Jessie is Max's late wife and the mother of Teddy, Lenny, and Joey. Though she never appears in the play, she is mentioned frequently and her presence is felt throughout. She is praised by Max in saintly terms as being "the backbone of the family" and also condemned by him as a "slutbitch." She had a close relationship with Max's friend MacGregor.

Joey

Joey is a rather stupid man in his mid-twenties and the youngest of the three sons. He wants to be a professional boxer and to that end works out in a gym. His regular job is as a demolition laborer. Joey is delighted when he sees Ruth and Lenny dancing and kissing and immediately takes Ruth to the sofa where he begins to "make love" to her. Later, he spends two hours with Ruth alone in his room but does not "get all the way," and he seems content with that. At the end of the play, Joey sits at Ruth's feet like a child, with her stroking his head like a pet.

Lenny

Lenny is in his early thirties and is the second son. He is a successful pimp with a string of prostitutes. Lenny is the first of the sons introduced in the play, and he seems to dominate the household with a cold, quick wit. He is also the first of the family to meet Ruth, and he immediately attempts to dominate her. He tells two long stories, one about being propositioned by a prostitute by the harbor front and the other about going to help an old lady; both end with his beating the women. Ironically, Lenny seems to be sexually as well as emotionally impotent; Ruth almost instinctively recognizes this and turns it against him. Lenny later suggests setting up Ruth as a prostitute so she can pay her own way while "staying with the family." At the end of the play, Lenny is standing to one side as Joey sits at Ruth's feet and Max crawls towards her begging for a kiss.

Mac

See MacGregor

MacGregor

MacGregor, now dead, was a ruffian friend of Max. Together they were "two of the worst hated men in the West End." Like Jessie, he never appears in the play but is often referred to and figures prominently in Max's memory. Metaphorically, MacGregor's ghost haunts Max because of Mac's "close relationship" with Max's wife Jessie.

Max

Max is the seventy-year-old father of the household. He is a shrewd, crude, brutish retired butcher. He attempts to maintain household dominance with threats and the evidence of his past as a hard-working man who supported his wife and sons. He also invokes his past reputation as a violent thug who was feared by everyone. His initial confrontation with Lenny at the beginning of the play ends with the father backing down from his threats. He later physically assaults both his son Joey and his brother Sam. Although he is viciously insulting upon first meeting Ruth, calling her a "smelly scrubber" and a "pox-ridden slut," he later speaks of her in sentimentally glowing terms. He is astute enough to recognize, near the end of the play, that it is Ruth who will "make use of us," rather than the other way around.

Ruth

Ruth is Teddy's wife and the mother of their three boys. She is the agent for change in the power struggle of the all-male household. Her marriage is apparently rocky at best. When she first appears in the second scene of the play, she immediately displays her independence. She uses semantic quibbles to undermine her husband's authority. It is nearly midnight and although she says she is tired and asks if she can sit, when Teddy tells her to sit she refuses to do so. When he suggests they go to bed she decides to go for a walk. Throughout the play she is able to take control from each of the men, beginning with a wonderfully understated theatrical scene with Lenny. She charms Sam and uses sex to dominate Joey. When the family suggests that she stay with them and help pay her way by spending a couple of hours a night in a West End flat, she knows immediately what they are proposing. She treats the offer purely as a business proposition and proves a tough negotiator. The men agree to all of her demands, and she agrees that it is a very attractive idea. At the end of the play she has chosen to stay with the family.

Sam

Sam is Max's brother and co-owner of the house. He works as a chauffeur for a car rental service. Sam is the only one who does not attempt to control Ruth. He seems to be a gentle, sensitive, and even gallant man. He is gracious with Ruth, and he tries to console Teddy by telling him that he was always his mother's favorite. There are many indications that he is not interested in sex at all, something that is used against him by Max. However, Sam has survived in this household; in his own quiet way, he is tough. Near the end of the play he attempts to undermine Max by blurting out what everyone has always suspected, that MacGregor had Jessie in the back seat of his cab and thus may be the father of at least one of the boys.

Teddy

Teddy, in his mid-thirties and the eldest son, is a Ph.D. who teaches philosophy at a university in America. He married Ruth just before leaving for America six years before the play begins. He has never told his family he was married, and, as the play begins, he is bringing Ruth home to meet them for the first time. It is soon obvious that the marriage is a dry and loveless one. Teddy is able to see what is happening in the dynamics between Ruth and the men of his family, but he is either unable or unwilling to put a stop to it. He has narrowed his intellectual focus in order to objectify others in an apparent attempt to avoid emotional involvement and thus to protect himself from pain. He says that he can see what others do, that it is the same things that he does, but that he won't be involved in it. He relates the family's proposition to Ruth and does not try to dissuade her when she accepts it. He says that he and their boys can manage until she comes back to America.

Media Adaptations

- *The Homecoming* was made into a film in 1973 for the American Film Theatre production series. It was directed by Sir Peter Hall and featured the original Royal Shakespeare Company cast: Vivian Merchant as Ruth, Michael Jayston as Teddy, Paul Rogers as Max, Cyril Cusack as Sam, Ian Holm as Lenny, and Terrence Rigby as Joey.

Themes

Alienation and Loneliness

A family lives in the same house and though they live side-by-side physically, their emotional alienation and consequent loneliness is palpable. Perhaps the most alienated of all the characters are Teddy and Ruth. They seem to have *chosen* to remain emotionally separate from the others. Teddy very clearly states this when talking about his "critical works." He says that it is a question of how far one can operate *on* things and not *in* things. He has chosen not to be emotionally involved with anyone and apparently has chosen to specialize in a very arcane branch of philosophy in order to maintain what he calls his "intellectual equilibrium"; more likely this field allows him to work with little contact with others. Teddy says his relatives are just objects and, "You just . . . move about. I can observe it. I can see what you do. It's the same as I do. But you're lost in it. You won't get me being. . . . I won't be lost in it." Teddy displays a near complete apathy to the events that unfold during his visit. Despite losing his wife to his father and brothers (not to mention a life of prostitution), despite watching his uncle collapse in front of him, he remains passionless and isolated from an emotional tie to these events.

Topics for Further Study

- Pinter believes that social violence is due to resentment. Research the break-up of the former Yugoslavia (Bosnia-Herzegovina), or other areas of late-twentieth century civil strife (such as Rwanda). Consider what part long-standing resentments played in the events. Compare them to the personal strife that occurs in Pinter's play.

- Research the feminist movement of the 1960s and after. Does Ruth answer the feminist definition of a free woman? Or is she a man's (Pinter's) idea of a free woman?

- "Subtext" is usually defined as "the action beneath the words," or as "the words *not* spoken." In *The*

Homecoming, compare what is being talked about, *how* it is being talked about, and the subtext in the first scene of Act II.

- There are many instances of events that are remembered in *The Homecoming*, such as Ruth's memories of her past profession as a model, Lenny's memories of meeting a woman down by the docks, and Max's memories of Jessie. How accurately do you think these memories reflect the past and how are they used to affect the current situation?

- Ruth in *The Homecoming* and Kate in *Old Times* both end up in control of their situations. Compare and contrast how they achieve these positions of power. What part does "selective memory" play in these power struggles?

Ruth also chooses to treat others as "objects" to be controlled. She agrees to work as a prostitute, which by nature requires a lack of emotional involvement, and at the same time she agrees to "take on" the men of the family. She shows no hesitation or sense of loss when she chooses not to return to her three sons and her home in America. She even calls Teddy "Eddy" when telling him not to become a stranger as he leaves for America.

Anger and Hatred

Anger abounds in *The Homecoming*. The play opens with Max looking for scissors and Lenny ignoring him. Lenny then responds with, "Why don't you shut up, you daft prat?" Throughout the first scene, as the family of men are introduced, anger and hatred seem to be the main traits of their relationships and their preferred modes of conduct. Lenny calls Max a "stupid sod," and Max responds with, "Listen! I'll chop your spine off, you talk to me like that!" Even when talking about the past, Max recalls that he and his late friend Mac (MacGregor) were two of the "worst hated men in the West End"; even something like nostalgia, which is typically happy and fond, is tainted with loathing.

None of the relationships in the play are warm and caring. When Max's brother Sam comes home from work, Max taunts him, and the seemingly gentle Sam retorts with innuendoes about Max's late wife Jessie and his friend Mac—a sore spot that has obviously been picked at many times before. In fact, the smoldering anger over the suspicion of what took place between Jessie and Mac is a weapon often used against Max by both Sam and Lenny. When Joey, Max's dullard younger son, returns home from the gym, Max turns on him and belittles his dreams of becoming a professional boxer. Joey is too slow witted to respond and simply retreats from the room. The attempt to escape from this seething anger and vicious attacks was probably what drove Teddy to retreat into a narrow intellectual discipline, to marry without telling his family, and to move to America.

Appearance and Reality

Although there are flare ups of anger and even violence, most of the brutality in *The Homecoming* is covered with a seemingly sophisticated veneer. When the actual physical violence does erupt, it seems comic. Lenny's stories about the tart down by the harbor and the old woman that he beat up are told in an almost off-hand way. The violence is contained in the subtext, the threat of violence to Ruth or any woman for whom Lenny takes a disliking. Ruth also behaves with outward decorum which belies her inner fire and sexuality.

Act II starts out with the whole family having after-dinner coffee and cigars. They exchange pleasantries about the meal, the coffee, and family chat about how proud Jessie would be of her fine sons and how much she would like to see her grandchildren. It seems to be a warm family gathering. Seething beneath the surface, however, is a violent dominance game in which there is a constant fight for control of the family. One of the rules of the family seems to be that when a blow is delivered the one who is attacked must not show his hurt. Even after Ruth has decided to stay and become a prostitute, Teddy's leave taking is comically conventional. He tells Max how good it has been to see him, there is advice on how best to get to the airport, and Max gives him a picture of himself to show the grandchildren. This surface conventionality helps to make the emotionally violent reality stand out as even more grotesque.

Doubt and Ambiguity

Pinter's plays are filled with ambiguity. He does not spell things out clearly and the viewer must often construct the past out of small hints, which may or may not be true. Lenny's stories about beating up women may be true or he may be lying to bolster his image as a tough pimp. It isn't revealed where in America Teddy teaches or if he truly does have teaching post. It isn't clear what Ruth means when she tells Lenny she had been a "model for the body." There's further doubt regarding Sam's sexuality, Joey's boxing career, and Max's younger days (though it is revealed that he and Mac were something of a fearsome pair).

Perhaps most striking is the dichotomy in Mac's recollections of his wife, Jessie (he refers to her as both a "slutbitch" and as a warm, giving mother and wife). It is unclear which of his recollections best summarized his wife—or if they are both accurate. When Sam says that he knows that Mac and Jessie had had sexual relations, he immediately collapses with an apparent heart attack or stroke and yet no one pays any attention to what, again, may or may not be the truth. Part of what

Pinter is saying is that life itself is mostly ambiguous and that people must often navigate their lives without satisfactory knowledge or guidance; the truth may set you free but good luck finding it.

Language and Meaning

Language in *The Homecoming* is used by the characters to attain tactical advantage. The language is seemingly a very accurate reproduction of normal speech. However, it is very carefully selected and, while still seeming "realistic," it reflects the fact that people think at different speeds, use language to evade confrontation, and think and speak in metaphors. Frequently people seem to misunderstand one another when they actually don't want to understand or to be seen to understand. Language, in Pinter's hands, is a weapon. Put into the mouths of characters like Lenny and Max, it seeks to hurt others. By belittling and verbally abusing the other characters, Lenny and Max can keep them off guard, control them. While this has been an effective tool in the past, the presence of Ruth upsets the balance. Not only can she match or better the men's verbal skills, she has nonverbal sexual skills which she uses to ultimately gain the upper hand.

Morals and Morality

One of the things that bothered some critics about *The Homecoming* is the complete lack of a moral framework. Although none of the characters seems to have any moral scruples at all, Pinter does not condemn any of them. That is part of the viewer's astonishment at Ruth's deciding to stay and "service" the family while also working as a prostitute. Equally astonishing is the calm with which Teddy accepts her decision. Pinter includes no hint of his personal feelings toward these characters actions. Their fates are stated objectively; it is up to the audience to decide what is moral and what is not.

Politics

At the time *The Homecoming* was written, many young British playwrights were writing plays with overt political messages. While Pinter addresses no political system in his play, *The Homecoming* does deal with politics: the psychic politics of the family and of the sexes. This play very powerfully shows these dynamics at work. By extension the audience is able to relate these politics to the wider arenas of organizations and even states. A viewer can easily extrapolate the relationship between Max and his sons to that between a politician and his constituents. Ruth's ascension to family dominance is, likewise, similar to a rebel force arriving in a capital and toppling the old regime in a coup.

Sex

The Homecoming is rife with sex, although none of it seems to have anything to do with love and little has to do with lust or pleasure. In most cases, sex in the play is another weapon used for gaining control. Jessie, the mother of Teddy, Lenny, and Joey, is viewed both as a nurturing figure and as a whore, a role that Ruth overtly takes over at the end of the play. Jessie's sexual relations with Max's friend MacGregor is a theme that is alluded to frequently throughout the play.

Ruth blatantly uses sex and Lenny's apparent fear of sex in order to dominate him in their first encounter. Later she again uses sex to dominate Lenny while they dance. Immediately after that she begins foreplay with Joey in full view of the rest of the family, including her husband. Later she spends two hours in Joey's room leading him on without "going all the way," and he is enthralled with her. She agrees to be a prostitute as a business proposition. Teddy seems to accept her sexual activity as somehow separate from her role as mother in their family of boys. Even Sam's lack of sexual interest is used as a weapon against him. When Joey and Lenny relate a story of their sexual escapade with two girls, it is really a story about having the power to frighten away the girls' escorts and then to have the girls in the rubble of a demolition site. Sex for these people is a matter of power and domination.

Sex Roles

Max has become the "mother" of the household in charge of the cooking. The men see women as objects to be dominated and to use for sexual gratification. Lenny runs a string of prostitutes; upon first meeting Ruth, Max assumes she is a prostitute; when Joey sees her dancing and brushing lips with Lenny in Act II, he exclaims, "She's a tart. Old Lenny's got a tart in here. . . . Just up my street!" Ruth is also the mother of three boys, as was Jessie. Part of what Pinter is dealing with, and part of what some members of the audience find astonishing and upsetting, is the fact that Ruth encompasses both of the stereotypical polar extremes assigned to women by men: Madonna and whore.

Sexism

The whole family of men assumes that women are there to be used. Teddy sees Ruth as a mother and helpmate. Max and Lenny immediately assume she is a whore. Moreover, Max attempts to lower the other men, attacking their maleness by calling them "bitches" or other derogatory terms usually used to refer to women. Ruth, too, uses sexism to emasculate Lenny. After toying with Joey she abruptly stands and demands a drink: when Lenny asks if she wants it on the rocks, she says, "Rocks? What do you know about rocks?" Her double entendre is not lost on Lenny. In fact, the whole play can be read as an attempt to keep women "in their place," and the victorious revolt against that effort by Ruth. She takes complete control. She escapes from a dead, arid marriage, and she takes control of the business negotiations and demands a contract based on firm economic principles. She will use her body as she sees fit in order to gain what she wants and without any concern for what others, including her husband, think. As Pinter said in a conversation with Mel Gussow of the *New York Times*, "Ruth in *The Homecoming*—no one can tell her what to do. She is the nearest to a free woman that I've ever written—a free and independent mind."

Setting

The setting of *The Homecoming* is realistic. It consists of a large room with a window, an archway upstage where a wall has been removed, stairs up to a second floor, a door leading to outside and a hallway leading to interior rooms. The furnishings, too, are realistic: two armchairs, a large sofa, sideboard with a mirror above it, and various other chairs and small tables. The set stays the same throughout.

Plot

The play takes place over a period of approximately twenty hours and there is one basic plot with no subplots. Here are all the requisite unities of time, place, and action that Aristotle put forth as the ideals for constructing a tight, powerful drama. Why, then, were audiences, including many critics, disturbed not only by the content but also by the form of the play? Part of the answer is in the audience's expectation that they will somehow be told about the characters in clear-cut exposition. In the realistic tradition—still overwhelmingly predominant in 1965—audiences expected to be informed of character background which would lead them to accept as ultimately logical and reasonable the responses of the characters at the point of climax and the falling action.

Viewers also expect the play to advance to its resolution in a logical cause-and-effect progression. In *The Homecoming* the exposition is slight and not always reliable because characters frequently constructs fictitious pasts in order to gain advantage in the present, as Lenny does when telling stories about brutalizing women when seeking to dominate Ruth at their first meeting. And, at first glance, most audiences are shocked and stunned when Ruth decides to abandon her husband and three sons to work as a prostitute and "service" the rest of the family. The denouement consists of Teddy departing for the airport and Ruth sitting in a chair with Joey at her feet, Max crawling and begging for a kiss, and Lenny in the background looking on. There is no further explanation for the action. The logical progression is there, but it is not blatantly put forth and explained as it would be in a realistic play such as Henrik Ibsen's *A Doll's House*. The audience is left to sift the action for clues as to how this outcome could possibly make sense.

Language

Another of the disturbing elements of Pinter's plays is his use of language. Pinter's characters speak with the all the hesitations, evasions, and non sequiturs of everyday speech. Moreover, the characters do not respond to questions with obviously logical answers, as would happen in a "realistic" play. Pinter's characters do not use language to communicate directly and logically; they use language to attack, defend, and stall while seeking out the motive rather than the direct meaning of the question.

Language for Pinter is never divorced from tactical maneuvering. He very carefully catches the rhythms of thought and language, and he structures these rhythms partly through his use of pauses and silences written into the script. These rhythms are also integral to the situation and relationships. While a great deal has been written about the use of these devices, they are not really mysterious to the astute actor: they are part of the thought processes. Pinter put it very succinctly in his conversation with Gussow when he said, "The pause is a pause because of what has just happened in the minds and guts of the characters. They spring out of the text. They're not formal conveniences or stresses but part of the body of the action. . . . And a silence equally means that something has happened to create the impossibility of anyone speaking for a certain amount of time—until they can recover from whatever happened before the silence." Nevertheless, to an audience used to hearing rationally logical conversations in plays of the realistic style, the more elusive—and more "real"— dialogue of Pinter's plays caused confusion.

Action

The answer to the problem of dramatic irony is that the audience must tune in to the action that is taking place on the subtextual level. Pinter's characters may seem to know more about what is going on than the audience because those characters are constantly involved in a battle for dominance or at the very least survival in the savage world in which they live. Even though on the surface the dialogue may seem to be about a sandwich or an ashtray or a glass of water, the characters are fully aware that the real action is about leverage, a battle which they can ill afford to lose. For Pinter, the shifting of an ashtray or the drinking of a glass of water is a large theatrical gesture. The characters know that, and the audience comes to recognize it as well.

Historical Context

While *The Homecoming* is grounded in the specifics of setting and family relationships, there is very little reference to the world at large: Nevertheless, the strife within the play's family reflects a turbulent time in the world in the year of its debut, 1965. The United States was being sucked deeper and deeper into the war in Vietnam. U.S. bombers pounded North Vietnam in February of 1965, and on March 8, U.S. Marines landed at Da Nang in the first deployment of U.S. combat troops in Vietnam.

Compare & Contrast

- **1965:** The feminist movement is getting underway, making demands for positive, concrete steps towards social equality and equality in the work-place for women.
  Today: While there is greater consciousness about women's issues and many advances have been made, there is still inequality for women in many facets of contemporary society. There has been some backlash to the more radical and strident of feminists.

- **1965:** The Sexual Revolution has begun, with sexual freedom being exhorted for both men and women. Concepts such as "Free Love" are advocated to free both mind and body.

Today: Society is more open regarding issues of sex. Sexual freedom in society is prevalent. Sexual issues are talked about and displayed in popular media that were unmentionable in 1965.

- **1965:** Sexual promiscuity is prevalent, with many people having multiple sex partners. Sexually-transmitted diseases, such as syphilis, are easily treatable.

  Today: There is broad recognition that promiscuity and casual sex can lead to incurable ailments such as herpes. The outbreak of AIDS in the 1980s brings the realization that sex can kill.

- **1965:** The United States, which has never lost a war, is one of two superpowers and is engaged in a "cold war" with the Soviet Union. The United States is also being drawn deeper and deeper into the war in Vietnam.

  Today: The United States went through a major trauma because of wide-spread opposition to the war in Vietnam, a war which the country lost. Nevertheless, the collapse of the Soviet Union in the late-1980s has left the United States as the only superpower in the world.

On June 28 the first full-scale combat offensive by U.S. troops began.

America in 1965 reflected the turmoil of the military escalation. Anti-war rallies were held in four American cities and the term "flower power" was introduced by poet Allen Ginsberg to describe nonviolent protest. The Hell's Angels motorcycle gang attacked marchers calling them "un-American." University enrollments swelled as young Americans took advantage of draft deferrals for college students to escape the expanding war in Vietnam and campuses were tense with unrest. Still more young men evaded the draft outright, fleeing to Canada to escape combat duty.

Civil rights activist Malcolm X was assassinated on February 21, 1965, in the Harlem area of New York City. The Voting Rights Act became law on August 10, and federal examiners began registering black voters in Alabama, Louisiana, and Mississippi. In Alabama, civil rights marchers were attacked by Alabama state police using tear gas, whips, nightsticks, and dogs. President Lyndon Johnson sent three thousand National Guardsman and military police to protect the civil rights marchers. In Chicago, police arrested 526 anti-segregation demonstrators in June. The

Watts section of Los Angeles had violent race riots beginning August 12. Over ten thousand blacks burned and looted an area of five hundred square blocks and destroyed an estimated forty million dollars worth of property. Fifteen thousand police and National Guardsmen were called in, thirty-four people were killed and nearly four thousand arrested. More than two hundred businesses were totally destroyed.

In other parts of the world, Rhodesia (now Zimbabwe) unilaterally declared independence from Britain. London called the declaration illegal and treasonable and declared economic sanctions against the country. There were demonstrations outside Rhodesia House in London. Despot Nicolae Ceausescu succeeded as head of state in Romania, where he would rule until 1989. There was a coup in the Independent Congo Republic and General Joseph Mobuto made himself president and proceeded to rule as dictator.

Despite such strife (and perhaps because of it), the United States was in a period of economic growth and prosperity during the mid-1960s. In his State of the Union speech, President Johnson outlined programs for a "Great Society" that he hoped would eliminate poverty in America. Across the Atlantic things were less rosy, as Britain froze wages, salaries, and prices in an effort to check inflation in that country.

The Federal Aid to the Arts Act was signed by President Johnson in September, 1965. This established the National Endowment for the Arts and the Humanities. The United States was the last of the industrialized societies to provide direct aid to the arts. In New York City, the Vivian Beaumont Theatre opened in Lincoln Center. Pop Art, as exemplified by Andy Warhol's Campbell's Tomato Soup Can painting, and "Op" art became fashionable. The Rolling Stones gained huge success with their song "(I Can't Get No) Satisfaction." The Grateful Dead had its beginnings with "acid-rock" in San Francisco. The mini-skirt appeared in London. The English Stage Company at the Royal Court Theatre declared itself a "club theatre" in order to evade preproduction censorship for the production of playwright Edward Bond's *Saved*, which deals with moral malaise and violence in working-class London. Off-off-Broadway theatres, founded as an alternative to commercial theatre, were growing in number and showing themselves willing to fight for freedom of speech and artistic expression.

In Hackney, a working-class neighborhood in North London just beyond the boundaries of the Cockney area of the East End, life continued much as it had for generations. In an unpublished autobiographical memoir quoted by Michael Billington in *The Life and Work of Harold Pinter*, Pinter vividly describes the Hackney of his youth: "It brimmed over with milk bars, Italian cafes, Fifty Shilling tailors and barber shops. Prams and busy ramshackle stalls clogged up the main street—street violinists, trumpeters, match sellers. Many Jews lived in the district, noisy but candid; mostly taxi drivers and pressers, machinists and cutters who steamed all day in their workshop ovens. Up the hill lived the richer, the "better-class" Jews, strutting with their mink-coats and American suits and ties. Bookmakers, jewelers and furriers with gownshops in Great Portland Street."

Critical Overview

When *The Homecoming* opened in London on June 3, 1965, Harold Pinter was already considered a major playwright in England, and his new play was eagerly awaited. Harold Hobson, critic for the *Sunday Times*, who alone had championed Pinter's debut *The Room* and his 1958 *The Birthday Party*, had said then that "Mr. Pinter . . . possesses the most original, disturbing and arresting talent in theatrical London," and he predicted then that Pinter would make his mark in theatre. The great success of *The Caretaker* in 1960, radio plays such as *A Slight Ache*, and short stage and television plays had fulfilled Hobson's predictions, and the word "Pinteresque" had already been coined to denote the playwright's style.

The Homecoming is a deeply disturbing play and the critics' reception reflected the drama's turmoil. B. A. Young of the *Financial Times* called the play "stark and horrible" but also said that it is "monstrously effective theatre." Although Young did not think Pinter to be an *important* playwright, he pointed out that "he has this enormous capacity for generating tension among his characters in which the audience becomes irresistibly involved." Bernard Levin in the *Daily Mail*, while crediting Pinter's "dazzling dramatic legerdemain," was negative and saw no point to the play. Philip Hope-Wallace of the *Guardian* objected strongly (and longly) about the lack of dramatic irony—in which the audience knows more than the characters on stage—and the fact that it was the actors (characters?) who seemed to know more than the audience. The critic seemed to be completely baffled by the play and said that it "leaves us feeling cheated."

Hobson wrote in the *Sunday Times* that he liked the play but was deeply disturbed by the lack of a moral stand by the author, saying "I am troubled by the complete absence from the play of any moral comment whatsoever. To make such a comment does not necessitate the author's being conventional or religious; it does necessitate, however, his having made up his mind about life." Penelope Gilliatt in the *Observer* called the opening of *The Homecoming* "an exultant night . . . it offered the stirring spectacle of a man in total command of his talent."

British audiences responded positively and the play had an eighteen-month run at the Aldwych Theatre in London before moving to New York on January 3, 1967, after a brief pre-Broadway run in Boston. It also quickly had other productions around the world: Paris, Berlin, Geneva, Gothenburg, Munich, Bremerhaven, Amsterdam, Copenhagen, Helsinki, Stockholm, and Sydney, Australia.

The Broadway reviews were mixed but predominantly positive. Norman Nadel in the *World Journal Tribune* called it a "nightmare play" and a "fascinating but unfathomable comedy" and thought it would appeal only to more adventurous theatregoers. Martin Gottfried, the powerful critic of *Women's Wear Daily*, found it "a fascinating and bizarre comedy" that "is so deep-veined with implication and so consistently provocative, controlling and comic that it not only demands respect but, more important, it wins attention and thought. The play . . . carries theatre life and with it the workings of a probing and creative mind." John Chapman of the *Daily News* did not like the play and, while he said that Pinter created interesting characters, comedy, and suspense, the playwright lacked the important ingredient needed to be an important dramatist—"good taste." The most devastating review came from Walter Kerr of the *New York Times*, who said that *The Homecoming* consists of "a single situation that the author refuses to dramatize until he has dragged us all, aching, through a half-drugged dream." He did find the final twenty minutes of the play to be interesting as Pinter "broke apart our preconditioned expectations to the situations" and "the erratic energies onstage display their own naked authority by forcing us to accept the unpredictable as though it were the natural shape of things." The general message from Kerr, however, was that the play dragged and needed "a second situation" to give it life.

The Homecoming managed to overcome the negative aspects of the reviews, went on to a long run, and established Pinter on Broadway. It won the Drama Critics' Circle Award, a Tony Award, and the Whitbread Anglo-American Theatre Award as best play of the year. It has been produced throughout the world and continues to achieve both critical and popular success in major revivals, such as that at the Royal National Theatre, London, in 1997. Pinter continues to be one of the most written-about playwrights working today, and *The Homecoming* is by general consensus held to be one of his most important works-by many accounts his masterpiece.

What Do I Read Next?

- Two of Pinter's early plays provide background to *The Homecoming: The Birthday Party* (1958), Pinter's first full-length play, contains all the hallmarks of Pinter's style and concerns; *The Caretaker*, which opened April 17, 1960, at the small Arts Theatre Club in London, explores loneliness and power struggles among three men. Centered on a tramp who is given a place to stay by a mentally damaged man, this play was Pinter's first major commercial success.

- Pinter's *Old Times* (1970), delves into time and memory, which Pinter finds to be fluid and uncertain. It also further explores the inability of a man to fully know a woman or to possess her. It is a move away from the more realistic *The Homecoming*.

- *Glengarry Glen Ross* by David Mamet shows the influence of Pinter, especially in the use of language, on the younger American playwright. The play was first produced in 1983 at the Royal National Theatre, London, at Pinter's suggestion.

- *Endgame* by Samuel Beckett was first produced in 1957 in French at the Royal Court Theatre, London. This play has some of the qualities and concerns seen in *The Homecoming:* mutual interdependence of characters, hate, an enclosed environment, and the use of spare language and lack of specific background information. Beckett is an acknowledged influence on Pinter.

- *Sexual Power* by Carolyn Johnston, published by Alabama University

Press in 1992, gives a feminist perspective on the American family from the seventeenth century to the present.

Sources

Elsom, John. *Postwar British Theatre Criticism*, Routledge & Kegan Paul, 1981, pp. 155-60.

Gottfried, Martin. Review of *The Homecoming* in *Women's Wear Daily*, January 6, 1967.

Grecco, Stephen. "Harold Pinter" in *Concise Dictionary of British Literary Biography*, Volume 8: *Contemporary Writers, 1960 to the Present*, Gale (Detroit), 1992, pp. 315-36.

Kerr, Walter. "The Theatre: Pinter's *Homecoming*" in the *New York Times*, January 6, 1967.

Nadel, Norman. *"Homecoming* Unfathomable" in *World Journal Tribune*, January 6, 1967.

Salem, Daniel. "The Impact of Pinter's Work" in *Ariel: A Review of International English Literature*, Vol. 17, no. 1, January, 1986, pp. 71-83.

Taylor, John Russell. Review of *The Homecoming* in *Plays and Players, 1953-1968*, edited by Peter Roberts, Methuen, 1988, p. 196.

Watts, Richard. "Hospitality of a London Family" in the *New York Post*, January 6, 1967.

Further Reading

Billington, Michael. *The Life and Work of Harold Pinter*, Faber & Faber, 1996.

> This is by far the best and most complete biography of Pinter. The commentary on the plays is extremely useful. Billington has been the theatre critic for the *Guardian* newspaper since 1971.

Burkmann, Katherine H. and John L. Kundert Gibbs, editors. *Pinter at Sixty*, Indiana University Press, 1963.

> This is a collection of essays by scholars and critics and gives a variety of views on Pinter's work as a whole.

Esslin, Martin. *Pinter: The Playwright*, Methuen, 1982.

> First published in England under the title *The Peopled Wound*, Esslin's book covers all of Pinter's plays through *Victoria Station* (1982), and includes a short section on the screenplays. Esslin provides great insight and a thoroughness of knowledge about European theatre that is matched by none.

Gussow, Mel. *Conversations with Pinter*, Grove

Press, 1994.

> This short book gives valuable insights into Pinter's working methods and his views on playwriting and life in general through a series of conversations with Gussow of the *New York Times* from 1971 to 1993.

Knowles, Ronald. *Understanding Harold Pinter*, University of South Carolina Press, 1995.

> Part of the "Understanding Contemporary Literature" series, this book offers criticism and interpretation and includes biographical references.

Lightning Source UK Ltd.
Milton Keynes UK
UKHW020633250920
370514UK00014B/1510